3617

Out of the Wild
The Story of Domesticated Animals

Also by Hope Ryden

Your Dog's Wild Cousins
The Raggedy Red Squirrel
Your Cat's Wild Cousins
Wild Animals of America ABC
Wild Animals of Africa ABC

Backyard Rescue
Joey: The Story of a Baby Kangaroo
The Beaver
America's Bald Eagle
Bobcat
The Little Deer of the Florida Keys

Out of the Wild

The Story of Domesticated Animals

photographs and text by *Hope Ryden*

Lodestar Books
Dutton   New York

Library of Congress Cataloging-in-Publication Data
Ryden, Hope.
Out of the wild: the story of domesticated animals / photographs and
text by Hope Ryden.—1st ed.   p.cm.   Includes index.
ISBN 0-525-67485-3
1. Domestic animals—History—Juvenile literature.   2. Domestication—
History—Juvenile literature. [1. Domestic animals—History. 2. Animals.
3. Domestication—History.]   I. Title.   SF41.R94 1995
636'.009—dc20   94-20763   CIP   AC

Published in the United States by Lodestar Books,
an affiliate of Dutton Children's Books,
a division of Penguin Books USA Inc.,
375 Hudson Street, New York, New York 10014
Published simultaneously in Canada
by McClelland & Stewart, Toronto

Printed in Hong Kong
First Edition
1 3 5 7 9 10 8 6 4 2

ACKNOWLEDGMENTS

Photographing animals for this book was a challenge. Where could I find my subjects? I began by looking through my old picture files. To my surprise, I found I had taken many that were suitable during my years of travel around the globe.

To fill the gaps, I visited the San Diego Zoo and the San Diego Wild Animal Park. There, such rare species as the bezoar and the Somali ass are being preserved, although neither species is on exhibit. I am grateful to staff members Joel Edelstein and Georgeanne Irvine, who made arrangements for me to go behind the scenes to photograph these special creatures. I located and photographed four other subjects at the Turtleback Zoo in West Orange, New Jersey, the Wildlife Conservation Park in The Bronx, New York, and Ross Park Zoo in Binghamton, New York.

Some of the pictures of horses, cattle, and chickens were taken at the Tillett TX Ranch in southern Montana, where I have enjoyed many happy visits. I wish to thank my friends Lloyd, Abbie, Gail, Latahna, Will, and Hip Tillett for their warm hospitality on these occasions. I am also indebted to my friend Buzz Benjamin for allowing me to photograph wild turkeys in winter through a back window of his home in Forestburg, New York.

Three photographs in this book were not taken by me. Two, on pages 23 and 29 (top), were contributed by the French Government Tourist Office. These are of cave paintings made twenty thousand years ago by prehistoric man, probably in preparation for a hunt. Although I once visited this very cave near the town of Lascaux, France, tourists are not allowed to shoot pictures there. The photograph of the Lapplander with his herd of reindeer (page 15) was contributed courtesy of the Swedish Tourist Bureau.

Finally, I want to express my gratitude to Dan Wharton, a curator of mammals at The Bronx Zoo. He directed me to excellent source material from which to write this text. Three references that I found particularly useful were *A History of Domesticated Animals* by F. E. Zeuner, *Seed to Civilization* by Charles Heiser, and *Grzimek's Animal Life* by Bernhard Grzimek. Additional source material came from the Ross Park Zoo, Binghamton, New York, and from the Munich Zoo in Germany. This latter material was translated from German by my brother-in-law Donald G. Miller.

Contents

INTRODUCTION

Did you ever wonder how it happened that domestic animals—dogs and chickens and pigs and horses, for example—gave up their independence and came to live with an alien species, namely us? How and why did this strange relationship between humans and animals come about?

A long time ago, the ancestors of the very animals we now keep in our barns and coops and fields and houses were wild and had to make their way in the world. Without help from man, they found food, raised their young, and looked out for their own safety. Chances are they were extremely skittish and took flight at the mere sight of a human being, just as wild animals—deer, squirrels, and songbirds—do to this day.

So what made them give up their freedom? Certainly, they paid a heavy price for doing so. In return for room and board, they now serve human beings in some not-so-pleasant ways. Many end up on our tables. Others provide us with hair or skin for cloth and leather. Still others perform hard labor such as dragging heavy loads or carrying us on their backs.

On the other hand, their former lifestyles must not have been easy either. Wild animals often go hungry. They also must endure storms and floods without adequate shelter. And they never enjoy total peace of mind, for they must always be on the alert for predators that hunt and eat them.

Nevertheless, nature has equipped every species with the ability to face such difficulties. And who knows? Perhaps the very challenge of surviving—of finding food and escaping from danger—adds zest to life. If this were not so, many more wild species might have traded away their freedom for the guaranteed food supply that people can offer them. For, of the thousands upon thousands of kinds of creatures that live on earth, only about fifty can truly be called domesticated.

Do these fifty domesticated species still look or act like their wild parent stock?

Some do, but others have been changed dramatically through man's selective breeding. By allowing only the most useful or productive domestic animals to bear young, man has created breeds that serve him best. As a result, today's sheep grow finer wool than did their wild ancestors; today's cows produce more milk, today's chickens lay more eggs, and today's dogs have more docile natures than the wild animals that gave rise to them.

By the same token, such breeding programs sometimes result in the loss of certain traits that serve the *animal*. For example, many domestic animals today are no longer capable of defending their young from predators. Were they to be set free, they would not survive.

How do we know that such changes have actually occurred?

In most cases, the wild forebears of our present-day domestic animals continue to exist in their original forms in remote places around the globe. By observing the behavior and appearance of this ancestral stock, we can see how their tame descendants have and have not changed.

In this book, fifteen domestic animals are described and compared with their wild ancestors. Each of these fifteen species was acquired by man at a particular stage of his own development. Prehistoric man domesticated animals primarily for food or to help in the hunt. When man learned to grow crops, however, he sought out more powerful species to work in his fields. Later, animals were subdued and trained for warfare or invited into villages to control pests. Finally, people discovered that certain species make interesting pets and kept them as companions.

Of course, every animal's story is different.

ANIMALS DOMESTICATED BEFORE AGRICULTURE

dog · reindeer · goat · sheep

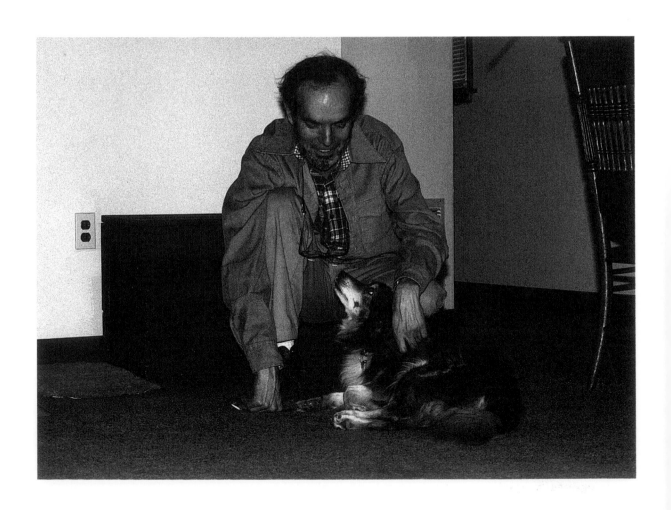

gray wolf

HOW THE WOLF BECAME A DOG

Before the dog was a dog, it was a wolf. We can be sure of that because the wolf and the dog are so closely related that the two species can interbreed. What's more, their offspring are not sterile but can go on producing offspring.

Today, only a few breeds of dogs still look like their wolf ancestor. That's because people have selected and bred dogs to possess characteristics that they consider attractive and useful. And since different people have different ideas about how a dog ought to look and behave, dogs now come in more varieties than any other species.

Some people think that the wolf adopted man rather than the other way around. Certain anthropologists who study the lives of people in undeveloped countries point out that feral (free-roaming) dogs often hang around villages, where they feed on garbage and kill rats. These dogs are tolerated because they keep the grounds clean. Something similar may have happened thousands of years ago with wolves. Perhaps prehistoric people allowed them to hang around their camps because they cleaned up old carcasses and rotting debris. When two species—in this case, man and wolf—serve each other, they are said to have a symbiotic relationship.

Can you guess what might have happened next? Perhaps children played with wolf pups born to the scavenging animals, and a bond was formed between wolf and man.

No one really knows when people first put the wolf-turned-dog to work. Skeletal remains of early dogs, found with manmade objects at widely separated sites in Asia, the Middle East, Europe, and even North America, have been radiocarbon dated to be more than eleven thousand years old. To have spread so widely, the dog must have been associated with man long before then. Without doubt, the dog was our first domesticated animal.

Meanwhile, the dog's wild ancestor continued to exist in its original form. By studying its behavior, we can understand how this animal, above all others, was able to adapt to life with a different species.

To begin with, the wolf is an extremely cooperative animal. It lives in packs, which number from three to more than fifteen members. Each animal must get along with all the others, for a wolf on its own cannot kill the large animals it needs for food. So every wolf is loyal to its own pack and valiantly defends that pack's territory. This, of course, is exactly how dogs behave with their human families. They are loyal to their owners, and they protect their owners' home and property from intruders.

wolf pack

Wolves are also able to keep their aggressive tendencies in check. Equipped with teeth and jaws powerful enough to crush bone, this predator must refrain from injuring its hunting partners if it is to survive. What differences arise have to be resolved peaceably. Whichever wolf holds the lower position in the pack hierarchy automatically gives way to the wolf of higher rank. Dogs act this way with people. They do not challenge their owner's superior status. They even submit to punishment without striking back.

Another way wolves foster good relations is by a show of affection. When two pack members meet, they greet with much tail wagging and face licking. Dogs behave the same way with their human "pack."

One final reason why the wolf-turned-dog hit it off with man is that wolves are smart. Pack members appear to lay plans before setting off on a hunt. Sometimes, several animals space themselves along a route and wait for the rest of the pack to drive a prey animal past them. Thus, as each wolf tires, fresh reinforcements are on hand to take up the chase. When prehistoric hunters enlisted the wolf-turned-dog as a partner, their hunting success surely must have improved.

WHY THE PEOPLE OF THE NORTH WANDER WITH THEIR REINDEER

The semidomesticated reindeer of northern Scandinavia and Asia and the wild caribou of Alaska, Canada, and Greenland are slight variations of the same species. To avoid confusion, scientists refer to both of these animals by their scientific name—*Rangifer tarandus*.

wild caribou

Long before *Rangifer tarandus* was put into service by man, it was chased and hunted by him. Paintings of the European caribou, estimated to be twenty thousand years old, have been found on cave walls in Europe. These were probably made by primitive people who were about to go on a hunt. Perhaps they hoped the pictures would bring them luck.

At that time, most of the Northern Hemisphere was covered by ice and snow, and life must have been difficult indeed for hunter and prey

wild caribou

alike. The European caribou, however, gradually adapted to this condition. Its fur grew thick and the edges of its hoofs became sharp, granting the animal secure footing on slippery surfaces. When at last the climate began to warm, the European caribou followed the receding ice cap northward to polar regions. There, to this day, its descendants reside, pawing through snowdrifts to feed on lichen and browsing on the willow and horsetails that grow in windswept, snow-free places. The descendants of these European caribou are now called reindeer.

To find enough to eat, reindeer/caribou must constantly be on the move. Even in spring, when fawns are born, there can be no lingering.

One-day-old babies get to their feet and travel north with the herd. In spring, especially, it is imperative that the animals keep ahead of the thaw, or they risk being eaten alive by the billions of mosquitoes that hatch on boggy, snow-free ground.

But how could such a constantly shifting, snow-loving animal as *Rangifer tarandus* ever be domesticated?

Some scientists say it never really was, even though it has served people of the far north over long ages. Others, however, do not see it that way. They say that the reindeer was the second animal to be brought under man's domination. And indeed it was. A piece of a reindeer sled that may be eleven thousand years old has been found in northern Europe.

Still, this descendant of the European reindeer has never been permanently confined by the people it serves. It migrates at will, back and forth across the vast Arctic tundra—trailed by people who rely on it for food, leather, and labor. For just as wolves in Alaska must follow the caribou herds, which are their main source of food, so the Lapplanders and the Sami people have attached themselves to the ever-shifting reindeer herds.

From time to time, these nomadic people hold roundups. Like

Lapplander with his reindeer

cowboys, they surround animals that they recognize as their own and drive them into holding corrals. There, they mark any young of the year that they have gathered with identifying ear notches; milk all the lactating females to make cheese; and kill a certain number of adult males for meat, fur, and leather. A few strong males are then selected to be trained as pack animals and sled pullers, and the others are turned loose.

Once freed, the animals quickly rejoin the great unclaimed herds that, for thousands of years, have trekked back and forth across the Arctic snowfields. For in this demanding polar region, every reindeer must find and paw for its own food if it is to survive.

GOATS FILL MANY NEEDS

Was the goat or the sheep the next animal to be domesticated?

Scientists aren't sure, for the skeletal remains of these two species are similar. Only if a horn is dug up along with ancient bones can a scientist know which of the two animals has been found. A sheep's horns grow

domestic goats

16

out to the side and then curl downward. Goat horns, on the other hand, curve backward.

Possibly the goat and the sheep were domesticated at about the same time. In any case, nine-thousand-year-old goat remains have been found in a Middle Eastern cave near Jericho. That discovery tells us that goats were being kept perhaps a thousand years before man began to farm.

At first, domestic goats were probably raised for their meat and to be sacrificed in religious ceremonies. As time passed, they filled other needs. Bags fashioned from their skins made excellent water carriers, and their sharp horns were used as digging tools. Then, after man started to farm, goats made themselves useful by eating unwanted brush, thus readying fields for planting. The most important function of this animal, however, must have been as a source of milk and cheese. Cows, it should be pointed out, would not be domesticated for another twenty-five hundred years.

The wild animal that gave rise to the many types of domestic goats we know today is called a bezoar. Small populations of this beautiful

male and female bezoar

creature still exist in parts of Asia and on two Greek islands. Unfortunately, it has been driven almost to extinction by trophy hunters, who like to mount this animal's horns on their walls. A bezoar's horns are indeed impressive. They are shaped like curved swords and are so long that a male can scratch his flanks with their tips.

This wild ancestor of the domestic goat has also been slaughtered in great numbers to obtain a stone that forms in its stomach. Uneducated people believe that this stone has medicinal value, despite proof to the contrary. It is nothing but a hardened hair ball, formed when the animal swallows hair while grooming itself.

One other problem threatens the small number of bezoars that still exist. Free-ranging domestic goats sometimes wander into bezoar habitats and mate with them. What offspring result are neither goat nor bezoar, but something in between.

NOMADIC PEOPLE DRIVE THEIR SHEEP FROM CAMP TO CAMP

Domestic goats are no longer commonplace. The same cannot be said for sheep. Sheep now number more than a billion animals worldwide and come in a thousand different breeds. They have displaced goats almost everywhere except in Africa. There are several practical reasons

why this is so. In addition to providing milk and meat, sheep also produce enormous quantities of fleece, which can be spun into fine wool or pressed into felt. What's more, sheep, unlike goats, are able to pant and so can be raised in extremely hot climates.

Some scientists suspect that human beings discovered how to press fleece into felt even before the idea occurred to them to keep sheep. The fluffy stuff is shed annually by the ancestor of today's sheep, the wild mouflon. In fact, masses of it can

female and male mouflon

be picked off bushes wherever this animal grazes. It is easy to see how the gathering of fleece might have led to the gathering of the animal that grows this wool.

Today, wild mouflon still exist in parts of Europe, Asia, and the Middle East. Their behavior offers a clue as to how man brought them under his control. Like their sheep descendants, mouflon are highly social animals that live in flocks. Each flock is inclined to move as a unit under the leadership of a dominant animal (even when the outcome may be disastrous). Such a follow-the-leader creature fit perfectly into the lifestyle of the wandering tribes who first domesticated it. With the help of dogs, these nomadic people from northern Persia (now Iran) were able to keep their mouflon-turned-sheep in tow as they moved from place to place.

Today, nearly nine thousand years later, dogs still help sheep owners to guard and herd their flocks.

ANIMALS DOMESTICATED DURING EARLY AGRICULTURE

pig · cow

GARBAGE ATTRACTS PIGS TO
EARLY HUMAN SETTLEMENTS

Dogs are no help with pigs, though. Pigs won't be herded about. They are too independent and also too smart. That's why their wild ancestor, the Eurasian wild boar, wasn't domesticated until people stopped moving, settled down, and began to grow crops—about eight thousand years ago.

A recent discovery, however, suggests that the pig may have been domesticated even earlier—some two thousand years before man learned how to farm. At an ancient site in central Turkey, a large number of pig bones have been unearthed. Whether these belonged to domestic pigs or to wild ones that had been hunted and killed for

wild boars

food is still uncertain. Scientists will look for other such sites before making a judgment.

In any case, wild boars were probably attracted by the food scraps they found around early human settlements. When pickings were poor, they could root for grubworms and for insect larvae that thrive wherever garbage is left to rot. Wild boars and their pig descendants have snouts that are beautifully designed to dig for bugs. And in the process, they turn over soil, making it more productive. This rooting

wild boars

behavior has been put to other uses, too. In France, for example, pigs are trained to unearth truffles, a hard-to-find food that is regarded as a delicacy.

Probably, those semitame boars that long ago scavenged on man's garbage also spent time in the woods with their own kind. At least the females, or sows, must have, for they are highly sociable. Wild sows form large groups called sounders, which also include all the piglets and yearlings born to them during the past year and a half.

By contrast, adult males live solitary lives. Only in the rutting season do they congregate around sounders in an effort to attract mates. At such times, brutal fights erupt between competing males, and injuries occur. Fortunately, these tusked warriors grow a layer of connective tissue on their sides, which protects their vital organs from being gored.

The wild boar, like its pig descendant, likes to wallow in mud or water, and this may help injured males to heal. The main reason why pigs wallow, however, is to keep cool, for they lack sweat glands. What's more, a pig's hair is so sparse that the animal can even become sunburned. By coating itself with mud, it protects itself from the sun's burning rays.

Domestic pigs today come in a variety of sizes and colors and shapes. Some have pushed-in snouts; others have hang-down ears. Only a few breeds measure up to the seven-hundred-pound creature from which they are descended. Nevertheless, this barnyard animal has not forgotten its past. A stray pig living on its own will quickly fall back into a wild state. In a few short generations, it will even look like the Eurasian wild boar that spawned it.

THE FIERCE AUROCH BECOMES A PLACID COW

The wild auroch of old, unlike the placid cow it eventually gave rise to, was anything but docile. It was huge, standing six feet at the shoulder. It sported curved horns atop its head. Yet Stone Age people hunted it on foot and with primitive weapons. Before setting off, however, they created pictures of this dangerous beast on cave walls. Scientists believe that they did this to gain magical power over it. Their cave drawings, made twenty thousand years ago, can still be seen in the south of France.

From the time those pictures were created until the first auroch was domesticated, many thousands of years passed. In fact, aurochs would not be kept until people invented agriculture and settled down, for unlike sheep or goats, this powerful animal could not be easily herded from place to place. Only after generations of selective breeding did its offspring become manageable. And even today, cowboys, dogs, and fences are needed to move cattle.

Meanwhile, the domestication of aurochs proceeded slowly. Evidence from bones and pictures suggests that around six thousand five hundred years ago the people of Mesopotamia owned cattle. Gradually, myths about bulls and cows began to appear in cultures as distant from one another as India, Egypt, and Greece. Cattle-keeping had become widespread, and over the next two thousand years, distinct breeds were

zebus turning water wheel

developed, each type suited to the needs of a particular climate or people.

In India, for example, a form called a zebu emerged. This breed of cattle persists to the present, for it is well adapted to life in hot, dry climates. It can be recognized by its high shoulder hump and the flap of loose skin (called a dewlap) that dangles from its neck. Zebus are used mainly as draft animals to plow fields, pull loads, trample grain, and turn waterwheels. Where wood is scarce, their dung is burned as fuel. Though females are often milked to make yogurt, this cattle breed is rarely slaughtered for meat. Many people in India are vegetarians and regard all cows as sacred. Zebus, therefore, are even granted freedom to roam through Indian marketplaces, helping themselves to food that is for sale there.

Meanwhile, in Europe, other breeds came into being. Depending on the diet of a people, one type of cattle would be favored over another. Yogurt-eating people developed milk cows. Elsewhere, people developed breeds that produced meat.

In parts of Africa, people make use of cattle in yet another way. The Masais do not milk their cows, nor do they kill and eat them. Instead, they drink blood drawn from a living animal's neck. Their cows do not die from this procedure, any more than people die from donating blood to a hospital.

Considering how long various forms of cattle have served people, it seems unjust that man killed off the magnificent wild auroch that gave rise to them. The last survivor died in Poland in 1627. But two German brothers, Dr. Lutz Heck and Dr. Heinz Heck, were not satisfied to let it go at that. They reasoned that the extinct auroch's genes still exist in the many breeds of cattle man has developed. By crossbreeding various strains, they hoped to reproduce an animal like the original.

Perhaps they did. Many scientists, however, reject the notion that what these two men recreated is the real thing. Nevertheless, the Heck brothers' animals are on display at a Munich zoo and can also be seen in a wildlife park in Poland.

Maybe the lesson to be learned from this is to value and protect the creatures nature has created before they disappear.

Animals Domesticated for Labor and Transport

donkey · horse · water buffalo · elephant · camel

THE DONKEY IS PUT TO WORK

After human beings had discovered they could make a zebu work for them—plowing, turning waterwheels, and trampling grain—they probably looked for another animal to perform hard labor. And they found one. Around six thousand years ago, wild asses were put to work as beasts of burden. It happened in the fertile Nile Valley, where farmers needed help moving their crops to market.

wild Somali ass

At the time, three races of wild ass existed in Africa, and each played a part in the development of the donkey. Today, two of these races, the Nubian wild ass and the African wild ass, are extinct. Only the Somali race has survived. Its fate, however, is uncertain due to unrest in its war-torn homeland.

It would be a sorry thing if the last of the Somali asses were allowed to die out. They are beautiful animals. Their coats are a rosy gray. Jet black bracelets decorate their legs. Their black-tipped manes stand erect, like those of zebras. They make a striking picture as they prance about in the mountains of their native land.

Perhaps this animal's best protection is the fact that it does not compete with man for good grazing lands, but gets along just fine on a diet of thorny brush and sharp grass. What's more, it doesn't need much water. Finally, the Somali ass is sociable, living in small bands of ten to fifteen animals, each big-eared member on constant alert. At the

donkey

first sign of danger, an entire band will take off, led by a cautious old female. And anybody who pursues them will soon find himself stopped by an insurmountable cliff, which the surefooted asses have just scaled!

All these traits show up in the wild ass's domestic offspring, the donkey, and explain why it is so useful to people in Third World countries. A donkey can survive on poor food and little water. It also lives a long time. Yet, ironically, this species is often badly treated, overworked, and even despised. To call somebody a donkey is an insult in almost every language.

This was not always so. The ancient Egyptians were especially proud of the white donkeys they bred. And when donkeys were later introduced to Europe, only noble families were allowed to keep them.

Today, the long-suffering donkey continues to serve mankind. Besides packing goods, it draws carts, turns waterwheels, carries riders, and even gives milk. During the last century, it carried the worldly goods of prospectors who went west in search of gold. Recently, donkeys have been trained to protect sheep from predators, just as some dogs do.

This willing worker deserves better treatment than it gets.

THE HORSE BECOMES A PARTNER IN WAR

Once, a primitive horse known as a tarpan ran wild all over the Northern Hemisphere, and nobody thought to tame it. Certainly not the Stone Age people of Europe. We know from their cave drawings that they killed wild horses for food, just as they did aurochs. Certainly not the first Indians in America. They, too, hunted horses for food. (As a result, the native American horse became extinct eight thousand years ago.) Even

wild tarpans

the people of Asia, who had turned the wild auroch into a plow cow, made no effort to put the wild horse to a similar use.

Maybe the wild tarpan was too hard to dominate. To this day, even domestic horses cannot be safely ridden or put to work until they have been "broken." Unlike docile donkeys, every single horse alive resists man's initial attempts to make a servant of it.

Yet around four thousand years ago, somebody did break a horse. A bone of that age was unearthed in Turkestan (now Turkmenistan), and on it was etched the outline of a man on horseback. Over the next two thousand years, use of horses spread westward from Turkestan to Europe and southward to Persia. Ancient vases found in those places show scenes of horses pulling war chariots.

From these artifacts we know that the first domestic horses were used primarily for war. We also know that they still looked much like their forebear, the wild tarpan. Only their flowing manes suggest that man had already begun to breed horses for traits that he liked. The tarpan's mane was erect.

It would be interesting to compare today's horses directly to the tarpan, if that were possible. Regrettably, the last member of that species died in a Polish zoo in 1851. Though efforts have been made to bring it back through breeding programs (as was tried with the auroch), the animal that has resulted cannot be called a true tarpan.

Fortunately, there is a second part to this story. In China, around four thousand years ago, another type of wild horse was being domesticated. This desert *equine,* although closely related to the tarpan, was larger and stronger and sand-colored instead of mouse-gray. There is good evidence that the well-to-do noblemen who first domesticated it held it in high esteem. An ancient cemetery has been found that contains the bones of hundreds of horses, as well as the chariots they once pulled.

But what of its wild form? Does that animal still exist?

For many years, this desert-loving wild horse was thought to be extinct. Then in 1870, a Russian army officer by the name of Nikolai Przewalski spotted a herd of yellow horses along the border of China and Mongolia. Soon afterward, zoological expeditions set out to capture and study them. It was quickly determined that these Przewalski's horses (as they came to be called) could not simply be escaped animals belonging to local tribesmen. For one thing, they all had erect manes—a primitive trait. They had to be a remnant population of the domestic horse's second ancestor.

Przewalski's horses

Today, zoos all over the world are breeding Przewalski's for future release. In 1994, twenty were sent to Mongolia, where they once again run free.

BIG-FOOTED WATER BUFFALO WORK IN HEAVY MUD

Even while tarpans were learning to pull chariots, still another animal was being brought under man's control. It was the water buffalo, a large beast with curved horns that is native to India and Southeast Asia.

This animal had one serious drawback. It lacked sweat glands and could not exist far from water. To cool down, it had to enter a river or a swamp during the heat of the day. But this drawback had a positive side. Having lounged in rivers and swamps over long ages, the water buffalo had evolved feet that could walk in heavy muck. This feature was important to people who made their living in swampy places. What other animal could work where the rainy season lasted for months?

wild water buffalo cow and calf

As things turned out, the water buffalo proved a most cooperative draft animal. Stronger than a zebu, it was also more gentle. Despite its large horns, which measured up to five feet from tip to tip, it was docile enough for an eight-year-old child to lead and even ride. And it was resistant to swamp diseases that infected other domestic animals such as cattle.

Some people believe that the water buffalo was first domesticated in Ceylon (recently renamed Sri Lanka). Others say it happened in India. Wherever the event took place, use of this animal quickly spread throughout tropical Asia. Even in southern China, water buffalo gradually replaced zebus, performing such tasks as pulling carts and milling grain. And in Vietnam, Indonesia, and Japan, wherever rice became a major crop, the water buffalo was indispensable. It willingly tilled flooded fields, readying them for planting.

Today, this powerful draft animal continues to be important to people in the Far East. The fact that it must stop work for a daily wallow

domestic water buffalo

does not seem to bother farmers. They simply lead their water-loving buffalo to wet places, where they can enjoy a good soak.

ASIAN ELEPHANTS ARE RECRUITED
TO CLEAR FORESTS

How puny human beings ever managed to capture and subdue elephants and then make willing partners out of them is beyond imagining. Even today, with the help of vehicles and walkie-talkies, it takes two thousand men and fifty tame elephants several weeks just to surround a wild herd and drive it into a heavily reinforced pen. Such an undertaking surely was more difficult four thousand five hundred years ago.

Yet relics from that long-ago time—engravings on coins and vases and buildings—show elephants performing heavy labor for their human captors. Not only are they pictured uprooting trees with their trunks, they are also shown carrying warriors into battle and, afterward, taking part in victory processions. Today, in parts of India, Thailand, and Sri Lanka, elephants still perform some of these services: They clear forests and march in parades.

domestic elephant

Of course, if wild elephants were not cooperative by nature, people would not have been able to train them. Wild elephants willingly follow a lead cow. When she signals danger by flapping her ears, the entire herd forms a protective circle around all the calves. When she signals that it is time to stop splashing about in a river, the herd obediently moves up on the bank. And every cow in a herd takes a turn at watching all the calves, while the other mothers browse. This cooperative spirit, when directed toward human beings, is what makes the elephant such a valuable partner.

wild Asian elephants

It is important to recognize that there are two kinds of elephants in the world: the small-eared Asian elephant, with a sloping back, and the large-eared African elephant, with a straight back. Both species are highly sociable and intelligent. Both species can be seen in zoos and circuses. Today, however, only the Asian elephant works for man.

wild African elephant

This, in part, accounts for the Asian elephant's decline, for throughout its long history as a working animal it has seldom been bred in captivity. When replacement workers are needed, hunts are organized and wild elephants captured. These new recruits are then turned over to professional handlers, or mahouts, to be broken and trained. So skilled are the mahouts that they can even teach elephants to obey commands that are shouted from a distance. It is amazing to hear a mahout call out "Lift the chain" or "Smash the tree" and then see the elephant do just that!

It is too bad that many people do not look upon the elephant with the gratitude and admiration that it deserves. Thousands of these gentle beasts are killed every year for their ivory tusks. At the same time, habitat that is needed by both the African and the Asian elephant is rapidly being converted to man's use. It is ironic that, in Asia, elephants are made to assist in this process—uprooting jungles that are needed by their wild relatives.

TWO KINDS OF CAMELS PROVIDE TRANSPORT ACROSS DESERTS

When did man begin riding camels?

The earliest reference to the domestic camel is found in a Bible story. It recounts how Abraham sent his servant to Mesopotamia, laden with gold and silver *and leading ten camels!* These precious gifts were exchanged for a bride for Isaac, Abraham's beloved son. This four-thousand-year-old story tells us that the camel was domesticated at least that many years ago. It also informs us that camels were prized by the first people who possessed them.

At that time, the camel may have been regarded as a kind of novelty. Cattle, donkeys, horses, and water buffalo had long been known in the Middle East and Asia. It makes you wonder what need man had for yet another labor-saving animal. What service could a camel offer that a zebu or a donkey did not already perform? Besides, the keeping of camels presented difficulties. The animal is a slow breeder. Females give

dromedary camel

dromedary camel

birth only at three-year intervals, and then to just one calf. To complicate matters, camels do not like being penned. When angered, they spit. Moreover, they smell bad—not only to people but to other animals as well.

Yet, to desert tribes, the camel became indispensable. Its broad, thick-padded feet were perfectly adapted to walk on burning, shifting sand. Double rows of lashes protected its eyes from the glare of the desert sun. It could even close its nostrils during a sandstorm. As for food, a camel can subsist on the poorest vegetation. And because it sweats very little, it is able to travel one hundred days without a drink of water. What better animal could there be to carry goods and people across desert countries?

Actually, two types of camels exist, and both have been domesti-

bactrian camel nursing young

cated. The single-humped camel is called a dromedary. It evolved along the borders of the Sahara Desert and therefore is able to withstand high temperatures. This camel was first domesticated in what is now Saudi Arabia. Unfortunately, its wild parent stock has become extinct.

The other type of camel has two humps and is called a bactrian. Bactrian camels evolved on the cold steppes of Central and Northern Asia, where winter temperatures drop to minus twenty degrees Fahrenheit. During these months, the bactrian's thick, shaggy coat provides warmth. When temperatures rise in spring, however, it sheds its heavy hair, which Asian people then gather and weave into blankets and clothing.

To this day, domesticated bactrians continue to transport goods across the hot and cold deserts of Asia. It is thought that this camel's ancestral stock may still exist in remote parts of Outer Mongolia.

ANIMALS DOMESTICATED FOR SPORT AND RELIGIOUS RITES

chicken

FIGHTING CHICKENS ARE KEPT BY MAN

Probably, the red jungle fowl's arrogant behavior was what first prompted people of northern India to capture and domesticate it; for in the beginning, the ancestor of the chicken was not raised for food but was kept for sport and religious reasons. Engravings of fighting cocks decorate four-thousand-year-old coins, and writings from this early

time sing praises to the male chicken, or rooster, for his courage and pride. Some even refer to him as the guardian of good against evil. As for the domestic hen, she was a giver of eggs. Who would want to kill a steady source of food for a one-time meal?

red jungle fowl rooster

One other piece of chicken behavior must have been attractive to people of long ago. Roosters get up early and announce the dawn by crowing. Since clocks were not invented until the Middle Ages, a domestic rooster's reliable wake-up call must surely have been a useful service.

It is interesting to compare present-day chickens to their still-living wild ancestor. At least one chicken breed, called the Bantam, has hardly changed. Even after four thousand years of domestication, Bantam roosters are as colorful, noisy, and quick to attack a rival as their ancestral stock was. Bantam hens, too, resemble their forebears, and like them, they are extremely protective of their chicks.

But there are differences. Unlike the gorgeous Bantam rooster, the red jungle fowl cock does not *always* appear in his most brilliant plumage. His most beautiful feathers are reserved for breeding season. And, compared to a Bantam hen, the female red jungle fowl's comb and wattle are hardly noticeable.

red jungle fowl hen

These physical changes are slight, however, when you consider how drastically man has remade other breeds of chicken. Today, poultry comes in a great variety of sizes, shapes, and colors. Nevertheless, all chickens continue to behave much like their wild relatives. Roosters proudly strut and crow and fight one another over hens. Hens scratch for food and cluck for their chicks at the first sign of danger. And in bad weather, they shelter their downy babies under outspread wings.

At least the lucky ones do. Most chickens, however, are no longer raised on farms in close association with human beings. Millions of them are mass-produced in terrible conditions. Hens are squeezed into crowded cages stacked ceiling high, and exposed to constant light to make them lay more eggs. Often their beaks are cut off to prevent them from pecking one another to death. Throughout their entire lives, they have no choice but to stand on wire mesh, never knowing the feel of earth beneath their sensitive feet.

In some parts of the world today, roosters are still being raised to fight to the death for the amusement of onlookers, who make bets on the outcome. In our own country, however, most states have outlawed this cruel sport. In New York, for example, anyone who incites two animals (whether dogs, chickens, bulls, or bears) to engage in battle can be sentenced to up to four years in prison and fined as much as twenty-five thousand dollars. Perhaps the human race is beginning to outgrow its fascination with blood sport.

domestic roosters ready to fight

This shift in attitude may account for the increased popularity of such peaceful competitions as horseback riding and dog shows. Today, many species that were originally domesticated to perform hard labor or to herd sheep are being kept for sport and pleasure.

dogs competing in show

PEST DESTROYERS

cat

THE CAT FINALLY ENTERS THE PICTURE

It is surprising that human beings took so long to adopt the cat into their households (especially since the dog was the *first* animal to be domesticated). For some reason, however, the charms of the cat failed to attract anyone's attention until seven thousand years after dog and man hooked up together. When cats finally made their appearance, though, they did so in style.

It happened in Egypt around four thousand years ago. The African wildcat probably let itself into granaries, where harvested crops were stored and mice abounded. The presence of a feline pest-control squad must have been a boon to the Egyptian grain-growers. Most likely, foraging wildcats were encouraged to live and breed in the big storage barns. It is easy to imagine what happened next. Appealing kittens, born in the granaries, were brought home to amuse children.

African wildcat hunting

But who would have thought that within a short time these little cats would be regarded as gods? Soon, nearly everybody in Egypt owned at least one, which they treated with great reverence. If a pet died, its owner shaved his or her eyebrows in an expression of grief, and an elaborate and costly burial was arranged for the deceased animal (even by people who could ill afford to do so). Many dead cats were mummified and buried with mummified mice, which were intended to feed them on their journey to the next world. And woe to a person who injured or killed a cat. Such crimes were punishable by death.

African wildcat with kittens

For many centuries, the Egyptian government did not permit foreigners to carry their sacred cats outside the country's borders. As a result, the domestic cat did not appear in Greece or Italy for another fifteen hundred years.

Meanwhile, people in these and other European countries depended on semitame ferrets to hunt the rodents that ate up produce. In Asia, the mongoose performed that task, although its appetite for chickens and eggs often outweighed its usefulness. Both the ferret and the mongoose, however, were almost entirely supplanted by the cat as soon as Egypt dropped its embargo on this most endearing of all mousers.

Persian cat

By today, of course, pet cats have spread throughout the world and are second only to dogs in popularity. Twenty-six breeds have been developed to suit every fancy. Some have long hair, some have short hair, some have curly hair, and some have no hair at all. One breed even has flop ears; another now lacks a tail. But whether Siamese or Persian or just plain alley cat, pet felines still behave much like their ancestor, the tabby-coated African wildcat. They are superbly adept at hunting for their own food. They have extraordinary ability to lie in wait. They are single-minded about marking the boundaries of their living space with bad-smelling spray. They never forget to sharpen their claws. And they know precisely the right way to bring up kittens—just as if they still had to survive on their own.

As for the African wildcat, it is found throughout much of Africa, although it is becoming increasingly rare. One reason is that human beings have taken over land that is needed by this animal. Another is the tendency of domestic cats to stray into the wild and breed with their ancestral stock. The kittens that result are neither wild nor tame.

ANIMALS DOMESTICATED IN THE AMERICAS

llama · turkey

LLAMAS WORK AT HIGH ALTITUDES

Thousands of years before Christopher Columbus sailed to the New World, mountain-dwelling people in South America were breeding and using llamas. This gentle animal is perfectly adapted to life in high mountains, where air is thin and breathing can be difficult. From its wild ancestor, the guanaco, the llama has inherited an extra large heart, a pair of oversized lungs, and blood chemistry that can make do with scant oxygen. This animal can be put to work, therefore, where another might not even survive.

And so, it has carried goods for people in the high Andes for more than four thousand years and to this day is central to their way of life. One tribe in Bolivia recognizes and honors their debt to this important pack animal. Once a year, they give their llamas a party. At this happy event, all the one-year-olds in their herds are decorated with beautiful ribbons, fussed over, and then blessed. Afterward, the people feast.

Were llamas not well treated, they might not work at all, for this cousin of the camel can be stubborn. A male will carry no more weight than one hundred pounds and walk no farther than twenty miles a day. If pressed to do so, he is likely to go on a sit-down strike—drop to the ground and refuse to budge. It pays llama owners, therefore, to treat their animals with kindness. And most do. Males are not shorn of their wool coats as are females, for it is understood that they need this thick padding to cushion the burdens they carry.

male llama

wild guanaco

Females, on the other hand, are not asked to carry loads, so their thick coats can be cut off in hot weather. The shorn fleece is then dyed, spun into wool, and woven into beautiful blankets or twisted into ropes.

Meanwhile, the wild guanaco still exists in a free state in the Andean Mountains. Guanaco society is dominated by males. Each tries to gather as many females as he can capture and then defend them from other males. Contests over females are noisy affairs. With flattened ears and raised tails, two rivals will run at each other, screaming and spitting. On making contact, however, they rarely bite. Instead, they neck wrestle until one of the combatants is forced to his knees. The standing llama then declares victory, and the loser withdraws without being harmed.

Except for their color, llamas and guanacos closely resemble each other. Llamas, however, come in white, black, brown, spotted, or speckled; guanacos are always golden.

NEW WORLD INDIANS TAME WILD TURKEYS

The llama was not the only creature to be domesticated in the New World. The turkey is also made in America—in North and Central America, to be precise. There is no record of just when Native Americans began breeding this bird. All we know is that Hernando Cortés, the first Spanish explorer to set foot on land that is now called Mexico, noticed tame turkeys there in the year 1519.

Imagine the excitement in Europe when some of these big birds were shipped across the Atlantic and put on display. The turkey must have struck people as very odd, indeed, for it lacks feathers on its wart-covered head and throat. What's more, the skin on its throat hangs down in what is called a wattle, which is not only bright red but grows even redder when the bird gets excited.

The wild bird that gave rise to this improbable creature looks very much like it and still inhabits many of the forests of North America. Like its barnyard descendant, it is a ground dweller, whose babies are

domestic tom turkey

precocious—meaning that they need not be kept in a nest and fed. Immediately after hatching, they follow their mother about, scratching for their own food.

Wild turkey mothers are sociable with one another and often travel together. Since each hen may have a dozen or more chicks in tow, a turkey flock may number over fifty birds. By contrast, male turkeys, called toms, are usually solitary. During mating season they fan their great tails and strut about, making gobbling sounds, in an effort to attract females. When two courting toms meet, they fight. Their battles do not last long, however. Soon, one of the two birds will flatten himself to the ground in a show of defeat, while the victorious tom struts off. Thus, neither bird suffers injuries.

wild turkey hens

The wild turkey is not much of a flier, although at night it has no trouble launching itself into a high branch to roost. During the day, it wanders about on foot, feeding on insects seeds, acorns, and nuts. It has excellent eyesight and hearing and, at the first sign of danger, slips under brush or runs quickly away. Turkeys are so fast on their feet that they can easily outdistance a person.

Domestication has changed turkeys in only a few ways. Some birds have been bred that are all white. As for behavior, domestic turkey hens seem to have lost some of their survival instincts. For example, they no longer hide their nests. Nor do they control their chicks with vocal commands when faced with danger. By contrast, when a wild turkey mother signals her babies to take cover, her entire brood drops instantly out of sight. Not one makes a peep or a move until its mother sounds the "all clear." It would seem that domestic turkeys have been lulled into a false sense of safety by the poultry growers who raise them.

ANCESTRY CHART

DOMESTIC ANIMAL	WILD ANCESTOR
Dog	Wolf
Reindeer	Caribou
Goat	Bezoar
Sheep	Mouflon
Pig	Eurasian boar
Cattle	Auroch
Donkey	African wild ass
	Somali wild ass
Horse	Tarpan
	Przewalski's
Water buffalo	Wild water buffalo
Dromedary camel	Wild dromedary
Bactrian camel	Wild bactrian
Chicken	Red jungle fowl
Cat	African wildcat
Llama	Guanaco
Turkey	Wild turkey

With the exception of the llama and the turkey, all the animals in this book are introduced in the order in which they were domesticated. Scientists, however, are not entirely in agreement on this matter. I have, therefore, chosen to be guided by the opinions of Dr. F. E. Zeuner. As for the llama and the turkey, these New World domestications were accomplished at unknown times without knowledge or benefit of what man had achieved with animals elsewhere. I therefore placed them in a separate category at the end of the book.

INDEX